The Penultimate
SUITOR

Winner

of the

Iowa

Poetry

Prize

The Penultimate SUITOR

POEMS BY Mary Leader

UNIVERSITY OF IOWA PRESS ψ Iowa City

University of Iowa Press, Iowa City 52242

Printed in the United States of America
Design by Richard Hendel
http://www.uiowa.edu/~uipress

The publication of this book was generously supported
by the University of Iowa Foundation.

Printed on acid-free paper

Library of Congress Cataloging-in-Publication Data
Leader, Mary, 1948–
The penultimate suitor: poems / by Mary Leader.
p. cm. — (The Iowa poetry prize)
ISBN 0-87745-765-4 (cloth), ISBN 0-87745-748-4 (pbk.)
I. Title. II. Series.
PS3562.E18 P46 2001
811'.54—dc21 00-053646

01 02 03 04 05 C 5 4 3 2 1
01 02 03 04 05 P 5 4 3 2 1

FOR JOSEPH KRONICK

Not altogether lone in a lone universe that suffers time

Like stones in sun. For we do not.

—George Oppen

Contents

Acknowledgments

American Poetry Review
"Parting of Su Wu & Lu Ling" and "Portrait of Fritz Kreisler."
Beloit Poetry Journal
"Album of Eight Landscapes & Eight Poems" and "For the Love of Gerald Finzi."
Kiosk
"Series as Opposed to Sequence."
Membrane
"Impetus."
New Letters
"Madrigal" and "Poesia."
River City
"Contents" and "from *The Book of Brilliant Accoutrements*."
Salmagundi
"Skin."

"For the Love of Gerald Finzi" won the Chad Walsh Poetry Prize given by the *Beloit Poetry Journal.*

"Impetus," "Madrigal," "Portrait of Fritz Kreisler," and "Skin" appeared in *The New American Poets: A Bread Loaf Anthology*, ed. Michael Collier (Middlebury 2000).

I

Madrigal

How the tenor warbles in April!
He thrushes, he nightingales, O he's a lark.
He cuts the cinquefoil air into snippets
With his love's scissors in the shape of a stork.

Hear the alto's glissando, October.
She drapes blue air on her love's shoulders,
On his velvet jerkin the color of crows.
Her cape of felt & old pearls enfolds her.

How the baritone roots out in May!
His depths reach even the silence inside
The worms moving level, the worms moving up,
The pike plunging under the noisy tide.

Hear the soprano's vibrato, November,
Water surface trembles, cold in the troughs.
She transforms blowing hedges into fences,
She transforms scarlet leaves into moths.

Rowboat on the Seine

(After a photograph by Irving Penn)

She sees from behind: the dark-coated rower, the oars
At almost symmetrical angles; another near-symmetry:
Boat/rower/oars on the flat beige surface, and below
Boat/rower/oars, suffused. Considered from this point of

View, this distance, this light, or the haze, at first
One assumes that the boat is receding. But then you realize—
Right— you're way ahead of me— if we see the— yeah—
Rower from behind, of course: the boat's approaching.

This then, is what she is to be given: a growing
Of the dark coat-back, the boat's dark hull, its banded
Rim: narrow red / broad blue / narrow red: coming,
Reflection breaking up. . . oar-splash, loudening, close!

And what she is not to be given: his face, his body,
His mind, mating hers, that blurring, when apertures flare.

For the Love of Gerald Finzi

Spider Mums

Not these, I think, stroking
With my forefinger the outermost petals
Of the individual I have selected, I think: *Not these splayed*
Phalanges,

Cream and smooth, first out, now
Farthest apart, sculptural. . . Rather, it's the
Innermost petals that intrigue me, those in the formative stages:
Something in

The way they minutely
Grip, curl, they're preparing for something later,
They're enduring the tension, the desire to do something, somehow make
The part that

Feels the desire obtrude:
A young girl in her skirts squats to pet the cat
Who lies on his side for her, a kind of girl: lonely, adult. Often
I address

Figures I feel close to,
Sketching under titles like "Girl in Full Skirt,
With Cat," addressing in the second person feelings I know: "You wish
Your legs were

Stems of such slenderness,
You could twine them together, tighter, tighter,
Tight almost to the bursting point, tight as silk cord twisted into fringe
For velvet

Cushions, or draperies
Like those at 'Grand-maman's.'" *Something needs to squeeze*
Or be squeezed to extinction, doesn't it. . . {I name her} Julie? She says:
Yes! And, and

"It's nothing to do with
My talented mother or with my mother's
Talented men-friends, nothing to do with my pastel chalks, or with my
Violin

Either!" "No," I confirm.
"It's wholly outside those things, but it's something
To do, to do with gripping/squeezing/pleasure/pain, *like* talented men,
Like the chalks

Themselves, like the very
Paper, whether cream and toothy, or slick and white
To soothe the sharpest pencil, like the rending violin itself." Still
Chartreuse, these

Not-yet-tendril-like. . . I
Ply them, these inward petals, with my left thumb
Away from the center's minuscule round yellow rug, I feel their urge
To go right

Back where they were, so tight,
So inside-gripping. But I could tell them what
They better face: even the most secret vulnerability is
Obvious.

This Music This Drink

Is melancholy
Or rather
Strong, sweet.

Spider Mums in Majolica Pitcher

Story
Story
Story

"It Opens. . .

. . . a strong outburst from the
Orchestra, the bass line constantly rising
To twist the harmonies in new directions. The first entry of the
Clarinet

Pays little heed to this
Introduction, the solo part rather prefer-
Ring to move things along in a more pastoral way. Two more attempts
By the strings

To add tempest to the
Movement fail to stir the clarinet, which calms
The orchestra down to a rippling accompaniment, so remi-
Niscent of

Finzi's songs. . ."

Source

Alun Francis, Program Note, Compact Disc, CDA66001, Hyperion Records, Limited.

Water

In whose motions children make dance,
I wish you had prepared me.
Water, in whose several bodies wanderers wash,
I wish you would heal me too.
Water, in whose extremes, of steam, of ice, pain forms,
Why didn't you cauterize, immobilize my infant heart?

Now, you had better warn your best friend, the earth,
Better warn each vessel made of earth or shaped like earth,
"This woman may well abandon you."
You should enlist the aid of your enemy, sun-fire, saying
"This woman half wants you to blind her, obscuring
All manifestations to which she cannot but cling."

Dear Water, How I wish you would gather yourself together and rise,
Gather yourself together with thunder and together
Overpower my sole lover, the air,
Commanding him:
"Send this woman this hour no barrier,
Rain on slurry-gray waves."

Paper

The novel that isn't getting written.
Or that is, with glacial slowness.

I imagine you.
The eyes that weary
Windowward
The rains blue
The highway mists
The headlights that speed.

The sheets look whiter
Under the black-metal desk lamp
With its skullcap and its elbow
Crane
The machine
The watermark
The white bird flying
The poet Hart
The verb

I imagine you.

In January, clarinet concerto.
Opus 31.
In white January.
The novel that isn't getting written.
Not one letter.
Inchoate pen.
Ink marrow.

The little box the pen-nib came in says
Osmiroid.
The flat little bottle of black ink
Says Osmiroid.
The box the pen came in
Said Don't

Shake your pen.
But it's hard not to shake your pen:

The story that isn't
The story that is.

Tenacity.
I imagine you.

A shiver.
A tapped furnace.
The bed where one doesn't lay oneself down.
The bed where you don't lay yourself down.
And then you do.

Riddle

Tending to squatness,
                    my bottom is broad.
On top I offer
             his hand a curve.
Both flat and round,
                   I spread heat,
Marry what he draws
                    with what he breathes.
Curious, he lifts
               the part that covers
My opening, his fingertips
                         encircle its knob.
He picks his time
                by his own thirst

But too, by the sound
I make losing pressure:
Then doth he grasp me
up altogether and pour.

Possible Solution

A teakettle.

Majolica Pitcher, Lots of Scrolls, More of the Words

"It's late."

These Fuse

Whether their quiet lamps darken or burn, fuse
Doubly, if only once, surely

Desire must twin, span the single night, link
The two horizons— radiant— black—

Desire must bevel the moment these vanish
Into a mutual dream—

Alert trees, and moon-on-glade, reflections.
There— these are pulled

Toward each other, toward
Fusing forever his bellow, her scream. . .

If only on paper

On Paper

Paper, smooth, and cream, as
The longest oldest petals of the spider
Mum I glide along my lips. . . not despairing till made-up "Julie" asks:
"Does that count?"

Man in Top Half of Dutch Door

He stays inside for indiscernibility
Like tears beneath closed lids. Closed lids describe

A shallow scalloped border. The kitten's mews describe
A shallow scalloped border. Dusk erases chances, moots

A day, invites a second widening, of sight and sound and of
His need to convey himself: *expanding broad rotations.*

II

Sequence as Opposed to Series

I

This chapel (before electricity)
Knows beauty of darkness in this image
Because its photographer knows beauty
Of black next to dim castings of glass when

The sky stops at evening and the chapel
Is darkening, candleless, lanternless.
The wildness of the heart, seeking outlet,
Increases in the dark and the presence

Of God only makes it wilder, frantic
To gush at last, just kissing, to orgasm.
Like William Henry Fox Talbot, you buy
Paper, and where he took photographs you

Write poems. I have seen you in your top hat.
I have seen your mouth: wide, sensual, tight.

II

I say to myself, Don't read his poem if
It hurts you so. Don't sit, emporched, rocking,
Reading a young man's poem as if
It were yours, or, as if it were *to* you.

'You don't need an extra ache, my girl,' I
Say to her: Young Lady. Old Woman. Neither.

'But— what he has done is *so beautiful.*'
Yes but— you explode with future, too—. . . Too.

I'll write my best guess at the inlander's
Dance on the beach: "Pipers and plovers and
Further, pelicans, launch in a body
Because I run." *Distinct from the body*

Is the rim, so that the still shell can swirl,
And the swirling surge can one, still, streak, make.

III

Why? To diffuse the intensity of
Our second true meeting, we staged our third
Outside, the whole time on the weather's verge,
The salt-light. Less facile with language, we

Let other wild things take on the stirring:
That wind that kept sounding like rain, ravens.
The sleek bee landing in his bottle of
Orange juice distracted but did not stop him

As he read his poem in the same husky
Voice he uses to compose. And my turn:
The black ant traversing my manuscript
Distracted but did not stop me, nor did

The other bee hovering, nor even
His hand as he brushed the bee from my hair.

IV

He kisses Margaret. He knows when girls
Want him to kiss them. He can tell. I want
Him to, even though I am not a girl.
Harpists need their fingertip calluses

To stay hard; they can never go swimming.
Here, where the stream runs over the manmade
Dam, the ruin of a folly stands, limestone
That would seem even colder next to his

Soft skin. I pretend to say, 'I would like
To be kissed here.' I feature his answer,
'Yeah? We should try it.' I'm old, old enough
To be his mother. I've said, "I don't want

Some mother/son configuration with
You, William." He said, "Oh, you're not. You're not."

V

Later on to myself I "say" to him:
'Your device goes: Just as fall/winter are
Every bit as pretty as spring/summer,
In fact more so, so brunettes [like his "you,"

I.e., her] are every bit as pretty
As blondes, in fact [his Margaret] more so.
This is news?' At the time, I said to him,
"You have *got* to start thinking in *meters*,

Not *syllables*." His dedication to
Her reads "These words are yours." Bullshit, they're *his*.
Her words are what she [inanely] says. When
We, for real, discussed his sonnet, he said

"I stole that line from you." "Which?" "That 'Across
Your mouth.'" Listen, I was telling you: *kiss me*.

VI

How delicate— the matter between us,
The issue, sweet— the tip of your penis.

VII

Why? Because this happens merely unto
Air. You, I mean you, William. You write
Yourself down between one sleep and the next
For whom? Rain on your window, you see. Rain

On your rooftop, I "see." I, Catholic,
Willingly take your intellect to heart
But. . . The bed in the other room, pauses.
My streaking window's text I cast in words:

"Hazelwood"; "last tracery of the last
Chance I might ever want." I can't tell which
You are. Ephemera? Recognizer?
Don't you see that I long to fill you with

Erections, that I gasp to behold you,
Presbyterian, in pain of my own?

VIII

I wrote "it," I wrote: "It," wrote "It is too
Painful"— I did not write "I never want
To see you again"— I wrote "It." "It is
Too painful to see you, right now." "I," he

Wrote me back, "understand, I really do,
I'm not upset." *That* was upsetting. Where
Is your anger, Man? You have lost me, your
Great and former mentor! He signed himself

"Your friend," then first name, last name. Now when I
Walk the dunes, or go downtown for errands—
The post office, the store— my reminder
Goes: 'To avoid him will be hard but it

Will help me the most.' *Your rhythmic shoulders. . .*
He does not trip on curbs. He does not crash.

Love

[tear here]

Series as Opposed to Sequence

No. 1

The overall rhythmic profile
Of hills
Washes and alluvial fans
Would rise and fall over the entirety
Ledges of cliffs and steep canyon walls
Would rise and fall over the entirety
While chattering in their midst is a thriving anthill
There are these very large clouds that seem to tilt
He is looking up at the sky and thinks *there's an intelligence behind all of this*

No. 2

The desert is associated with
Preserving itself as long as it can
Dependent upon
Sustaining instruments
Hallucinations and insanity
A lightness and constant ambiguity
That basic ambiguity
Gray-green or blue-green
The possibility of not necessarily listening just to one thing or the other
Where there are no words at all

No. 3

When the structures begin
Sustained from the very beginning with very small slow changes
Usually comprising paired mallet instruments and sometimes two pianos
Each group is lightly doubled
When the structures begin
Where the A sections are slow and the B section moves up
Just after dusk
Each group is lightly doubled
And when listening in particular to two pieces
Primarily on one or two nights
Each group is lightly doubled
Fascinated by the symmetry

No. 4

Usually a single plant produces only a few flowers each season
This
Of course is
An old technique
It threatens one's normal thinking
The percussion is omnipresent
Clicking sticks
Just after dusk
They're pulsed
The realm of pulsation
To supply the ongoing pulse
The pulse which begins and ends
After about forty minutes
After more than a thousand years
A series of spasmodic jerks
He sort of reaches out
A wordless response to
Purely
Rapid eighth notes
This is an extremely emotional moment

No. 5

A vision
At 2000 to 4000 feet elevation
That you'd never get if the notes were sustained
Begins with this pulsation
Of available vibrations
Fruit red
Of the most intense and sophisticated sort
Ripening
In the desert or in grassland
Like strings or the electric organ
Repeating over and over again
"Fruit Red"
Gravel or coarse sandy soil
Sets up a kind of rhythmic energy
It's as if you're in the desert and you're running as fast as you can

No. 6

Gray-green or blue-green
Birds open the fleshy fruit from the side
Going into a text and then out of it again
That constant flickering of attention
All sequences
Simultaneously
Continued
Between what the text says and its pure sensual sound
A light radiating out of the dark infinitude
Out of this complete continuity
A-B-A
A-B-C-B-A
From beginning to end

No. 7

Reading his work to the present
With regard to where the stresses and where the beginnings and endings are
Dependent upon
The recipient
With the apical cup not prominent
But more chromatic and darker in harmony
Its own harmonic cycle
He then goes on to more complex pieces
With a few scales
Slowly
In the desert in a land belonging to no one
It is to this possibility that the words refer
And no more and no less

No. 8

Produced thirty-one flowers
Produced thirty-one flowers
Repetitive in any literal sense
In order to set up the feeling
Structure and harmony
The surrounding woody vegetation for protection from animals
Different things are happening at the same time
Or later if the weather is cool
Often move at a very slow rate of change
Are fast and use the same harmonic cycle
So the voices continue without words
With twenty-four open blossoms
Another plant on the desert at Sacaton was photographed
Normally over by seven o'clock the following morning
Another plant on the desert at Sacaton was photographed
For the lower part of it is brittle and easily broken
Another plant on the desert at Sacaton was photographed
And a single flower may scent the air for 100 feet

No. 9

But one unusually large plant in Tucson
Just after dusk
A kind of barge of light
Just after dusk
A large arch
Just after dusk
His death at age 80
Just after dusk
At which point the chorus sings "dee-dee-dee-dee-dee-"
And is itself an arch form
Without anything else added or subtracted

No. 10

Of hills
Of washes
Of alluvial fans
Ledges of cliffs and steep canyon walls
Late in May or in June
With a few scales
Floating down a river in very dark surroundings in complete darkness
Glissandos which with contact microphones attached
Resolved to put a plant of light in the last part
Between fascinated by the symmetry
Different from
The recipient
He sort of reaches out
A series of spasmodic jerks
The perfume is liberated in profusion

No. 11

Art

- -

[tear here]

Parting of Su Wu & Li Ling

The one in a ponytail, the other in a loosened tie; friends;
A mythic weathery day: rain from the west, and from the east, fog.

Friends: clothes and hair: present details; the breakfast they had together,
Past details: paper napkins, everything bagels;

The fact that from now on they'll have every meal apart: tiny future detail.
Over are each of the years when one would say, "I can stay a long time today!"

And the other would say, "Great!";
Gone are any of the moments when one of them could have said,

"I'd rather live with you. Why can't things be arranged around that?"
They are poets, and they will never see each other again.

Two poets, and they know they will never see each other again.
Both poets, and what they can think of to say is, "Okay," and "All right."

III

Album of Eight Landscapes & Eight Poems

The moment you meet a teacher, you should leave
The teacher, and you should be independent.
—Shunryu Suzuki

For what care I who calls me well or ill,
So you o'ergreen my bad, my good allow?
You are my all the world, and I must strive
To know my shames and praises from your tongue;
—William Shakespeare

- -

Too much, *too much*—
all this yellow in early
October, the way the yellow light
Saturates
all of the
not-completely-degreened
Leaves,
saturates
even the air *between* leaves—
The red sandstone promontory
oranged out,
yellow-gray for the gravel—
I swear
the sun's on the road
and just about every
Wildflower that's late
says yellow
millions of times
and leaves.

- -

How will I find it?
equipoise in tumult—
balance out of plunge—
I don't see how, how,
for you may not be but you seem to be
all thought,
A migration of monarchs in autumn
bright all-of-a-sudden gestures. . .

We correspond.
We correspond.
I can say
Any word,
can it
correspond?
And,
too,
the ducks, the geese,
Go or begin
to go
before the swirl and fall of. . . But
Not every
leaf
is finished.

- -

In the whitening
now of November,
I know, of *course*,
I know December in-holds
something firmer
something root-stocked, something
After.
But how many years will it take me?—
what years multiplied by what seasons

Take me? just to reword,
to enclose,
finally to
Release
just this one hour of you,
this one-of-the-last I'm allowed
To write to your knowing—
my pages flown to
your lap, that *far*.

This hour and too
the lake hour in September,
also alone, but you *were*
The water, you were,
the glittering white-light leaf-shapes
on that wondrous surface, laid over
The blue depth. . .
your eyes. . .
how could you see this:
You were *there*,
in the reeds in the cattails
green going to yellow to brown
In the wind in the wind
that was you it was you
and you bent—

Christ, I've had it with this fucking elegy
I want these fucking photographics
DOWN!
And I don't mean
leaf down in yellow or
aflame, afloat on pretty

Blue ponds in New Fucking Hampshire!
I mean not even brown but gray
and shriveled, shrunk
Or better, sunk
to bracken, rot:
I want
that pond
iced up.
If I can't have you coming, then
I want you gone. I'm Grown— *I don't*
want this—
HUGE LOVE
scaled
down.

- -

What good does it do
to note
aqua-gray sky, oak leaves
Soaked *orange*—
deep *copper*, the sun declining. . .
then the sky a momentary *paler*
Aqua still, trees forming
wrought-iron silhouettes out of
dullest orange, in the last rays.
Looks like Tiffany *lamp* light.
So what?
My grandmother gave me
A pair of *glass* candleholders—
turquoise blue—
"Depression Glass"— telling me how,
When my father was a little boy,
he thought they looked like
his eyes.

Once in a *fiery* spell,
I smashed those things with a board,
then cried
Inconsolably,
picking up pieces. . .
putting them in that *brown paper* bag. . .
A brown not unlike *these oak-leaves*.
Big deal. I hate all mirrors,
like myself in you.
Brown paper bags,
candles set inside them
in sand at Christmastime:
Luminarias.

- -

What is meant?
Sometimes I dream I'm in
the landscape,
Mountains,
steep blue-black, for
miles and miles—
Mountains—
mists— slowly rising, slowly settling—
over depths—
The bell and its necessities:
time and a hollow body.
And underneath that sound a sound
A drone
under the wind. And wind is always
skyward. . .

- -

Absolutely forced
to love absolutely
forced to this ending,

I find myself in your words:
"the double-edged nature of all
profound encounters,
Revealing and confusing,
regenerating and
destroying."
My heart feels
like an animal, a mare
lying on her side in a cave,
Brooding, sick.
And yet I cannot help but set my eyes upon
beyond— the grassy plains—
Being what I know:
those undulations. . .
I'd like to show how *different*
The yellows are— the autumn grasses—
some brass-colored,
some a near-white chartreuse.
I will show you this:
my deepest bow,
for you have taught me
The inside and out
are *just the same*. I bow—
before I dash— in your honor.

- -

Impetus

A man half Alan and half Uncle Arnold
Stopped by the millinery shop to mention:
"Cursed be any God who allows the old
To flop on this regular a basis." Shun

Any omnibus which is a tourists' tour,
Any present for the apparition of a Virgin
As in the Rinuccini Triptych's flames. Our
Tongues one by one by one by one cave in.

To get to the shop he went up a perpendicular
Road; the carriages had to be strapped to it.
He heard the dots in the park say, "No end
To this lot, they're all commonplace." I

Heard him say, "Right, but you err to be seeking
Minimal falls. Pastoral falls take flight:
You, Brook, release me, lift my weak king."
Back God comes, nailing horses' hooves to light.

Poesia

(In cui appare il canto dell'angelo della terra-cotta)

i.

The peacock of Santa Ágata tolls the evening
With his cry at intervals of fifteen minutes.
The dogs converse in the accents of agitation.
The motorcycles exert themselves up the climactic hill.
No pane, no shutter, no shade, no curtain
Closes off the sounds of this night, from me.
The trees, at a signal from the wind, air out their leaves.
The church bells insert commas in time.

ii.

Nor panes nor shutters nor shades nor curtains
Close off the nightly sounds, from him,
From the angel who stays in his niche, the angel
Whose curls the weather has worn into his ears.
Yet his ears have no canals, his eyes have no pupils,
So, it is up to me, alone, right now
'Mid this night of sound, to imagine what would be
"The Canto of the Terra-Cotta Angel":

iii.

I'm glad I'm no inhabitant of the other heaven,
That paneless, shutterless, shadowless place.
Glad, yes glad day and night,
Even when I learn how the drunken boy has broken
The window below. This way I have knowledge
At least of something, something of the human,
Something in addition to the permanent ache
Between my immutable shoulders.

Malleable Day

To sum up: the musical part: undulating horizontal lines, blue & orange harmonies tied together
By yellow & purple (which are their derivatives), lit by greenish sparks.—Paul Gauguin

I.

Skin
For the Love of Gerald Finzi
Portrait of Fritz Kreisler
Poesia in cui appare il canto dell'angelo della terra-cotta
Album of Eight Landscapes & Eight Poems
The Parting of Su Wu & Li Ling
Rowboat on the Seine

II.

Impetus
Sequence as Opposed to Series
Series as Opposed to Sequence
The Marrying Maiden
Depiction of a Game by Pieter Brueghel the Elder
Love Once Chiseled in Stone
Algorithm Exacted on Three Plucked Instruments

III.

Vibration
Snow on the Skylight All Afternoon
White Sands
Balm
Heavy Roses
from *The Book of Brilliant Accoutrements*
Contents of *The Harlequin Prints*
Red Rose & Blue Reader
New Pillowcases
Madrigal

Depiction of a Game as if by Pieter Brueghel the Elder

An unexamined life is worth living.
—The Author

Rules

O inexperienced relay that retables sequences
Reflections in the breezy air
Swifts and gyrations
Light , dews , flashed
Blue by day , red of bleed , then lazy quince
Essential as the bowl of silt
That tints the spin
That sinks in slumber , then , in death , O

Chits

🖐 🚶⛯❄|👓⌛❒✼🚲⛩❋🏛🛡 ❒❄✡❀⚓ 🗼✼❀☞ ❒☎⛩❀✏❂❄✂ ⛯⛪
❒👪?🌐⛪⚱✂✼📖❅🗼❄❋☞🚶❒✝🌐 🖐📖 ☞🐟❄ ❂❒❄?🚲 ❀✼❒
✳✏🛡❅☞🖐 ❀⛩❄ ✳▌⚱❀☞✡❒⛯✂★⛪✳🚶☞✌ ⛯❄👓✂ ✌
❅✝❀🚦✼?❄ ☎🗼⌛❄ ❂⚓ ❀⚱⛪ ✌ ❒❄❄ ❒❅ ❂🖐❄💻❄ ✌
🚲⛪❄⛩ ⌛❀▌▌ 🏛👪✼⛩❋🐟 ✥🚲🌐🛡👓🗼✼✏🗼 ❀✂ 🚦✼❄ ❂🏛◗🗼
❒❅ ✂✼⚱✐✶✏❀🚶 ☞✼🖐⚓⛯ ✡✼❄ ✂❒✼⌛✶✼❀☞
🌐✼👓✡✂ 🗼✂⛩👪🚲🛡❂📖🚦 ✌ ☞✼🏛🚶 ✌ ?🌐 ❄☎❀👓⛪ ✌ ☆

Chant

Airy day a stem THAT EASY ! startles out
Almighty Usurer separates out the sold from the given
O the yellow plums outshine the moon
Ooze all night and in the core (d a z z l e)
CAR-PAY DEEM CAR-PAY DEEM
(Taunt) (Squint) (Laugh) " Relay! " *SQUEEZE ye'r MUG o' CLAY*

Portrait of Fritz Kreisler

(Addressed to the photographer whose name is not stated on the reproduction in hand although the caption does supply the year the picture was copyrighted: 1913.)

The emphasis on the dull and the glossy
   surfaces, especially of the violin-body,
   which has, in this light and shadow, both; &
The matte of the violinist's cheek, his jaw, his brow, below
The gleam of his up-combed waves;
The flat wool of his coat, lapels & sleeves,
   setting off
The coin-like tie-clasp,
The medal-like watch-fob,
The strange lozenge of glass toggled on its long silk ribbon;
The emphasis on little things:
The ridge where his lower lip ends,
The violin's four pegs angled differently, catching
   different degrees of dim and shine, near and echoing
The fabric-covered buttons of his vest: both designs for thumb & forefinger;
The small things:
The clitoris inside a woman,
The shutter-button on your camera:
The places that open and close and tune and control.
Don't ask him to smile.
Don't ask him to make less specific
   the tilt of his head.
Don't ask him to move his right knuckles
   from where they indent his waistcoat.
Don't ask him to lift the violin and its bow
   dangling from his left hand
   and put them into playing position.

Don't ask him to avert that direct gaze of his, coldly
    assessing you though it is.
He would just as soon you did your job, accomplished
    this session with expertise and dispatch so
He can get on to lunch with a woman.
He does not want you to join him for lunch.
He does not want to have to come back and do this over
    so take whatever pictures you will now.
He looks on you more or less as a tailor.
He expects you to make him look good, but
He cares nothing for you, and is not curious about your work.
He does not see it as comparable to his own form of virtuosity.
He may— no, he will— he will notice
The crumbs in your moustache from
The cold roll you crammed into your mouth with your coffee.
He doesn't care.
He may, as small talk, describe your slovenliness to his companion at lunch.
He wants her to want him.
He will give her those intense eyes, his head cocked at
The angle he strikes
    habitually, as now, for you, habitually subtle.
    An afternoon— or part of one— in the Hotel Blank.
He will not fuck her in his shirt— he can wait— and prefers it naked,
    and under the covers,
    with his eyes closed, so as to smell
The perfume and the cunt, so as to feel
The hair massed in his hands, so as to hear
The every noted moan, because he is working on
The Sibelius,
The Concerto in D minor, and needs to fill it full of
    someone's longing for himself.

Heavy Roses

(After a photograph by Edward Steichen)

@ @ @ @ @ @ @ @ @ @ @ @

(1) Two in the afternoon, the village florist's cellar,

(2) In tubs, cool on the floor, three or four shades to a tub.

(3) They have no mirror, they have to ask:

(4) *Am I damask, or an older woman's blush?* "& I have

(5) Some yellow ones in the back," the shopgirl says.

(6) *Am I the crimson of veinal blood*

(7) *Or more like arterial blood, shouted on a suicide's sleeve?*

(8) "No, no," I say. "I'm confused enough as it is."

(9) *Am I simply unsatisfied,*

(10) *Or truly insatiable, as I have been accused of being?*

(11) "I am drawn to these," I say,

(12) & I watch the shadow of my own hand hover.

@ @ @ @ @ @ @ @ @ @ @ @

To be thumbing your heart, to get that drunk.
Rainless night in Voulangis, Full Bloom.

@ @ @ @ @ @ @ @ @ @ @ @

H -e --a ---v ----y
R -o --s ---e ----s
H -e --a ---v ----y
R -o --s ---e ----s
H -e --a ---v ----y
R -o --s ---e ----s
W -h --i ---t ----e
N -o --i ---s ----e
R -o --s ---e ----s
H -e --a ---v ----y
W -h --i ---t ----e
N -o --i ---s ----e
H -e --a ---v ----y
R -o --s ---e ----s
H -e --a ---v ----y
R -o --s ---e ----s
H -e --a ---v ----y
R -o --s ---e ----s
H -e --a ---v ----y

The darkness as my wedge
Petals like parentheses
Centered clusters
Thinking stems
Initiated from after
Planning ago
Their own moon-in-close-up light

After daybreak, heavy roses, heavy roses
Will dominate my lens

(Curve on top of curve on top of curve).
How wet will they still be?

Am I to be a priest? A voyeur? A
Callous murderer? A cold lure?

No, I am to be the father with clear eyes
Blinded by the thin & falling petals of heavy

Roses out of a windy night.

@ @ @ @ @ @ @ @ @ @ @ @

I decided whether to re-angle the most prominent rose.
I decided not to.
I decided that if I did trade the shadow for the light, I might not be able to
Get it back, & shadow draws out the invisible.
I decided the container was irrelevant. I decided the background was
Relevant but only if blocked out.
I decided to get even with my subject, I mean to say, on eye-level.
I decided Steiglitz was right when he said it wasn't getting any easier for me.
But then Steiglitz knows how to take a picture & I decided to prefer my
Struggle to his knowledge.
I decided whether to save any of my precious film to capture the Germans
If— not if but when— they reached Paris. 'Only 30 kilometers away.'
I decided not to.
I decided whether to save any of my precious film for Clara in the doorway,
Clara in the mirror.
Again I decided no.
I decided to remember the rose I drew, alongside my initial, as a signature to
The Mirror.
That time I did re-angle her wrist. & I am not sorry.
I decided that I would rather sleep in candlelight than in a darkened room.
I decided it should be the candles from my coat pocket, downy with wool
Filaments.
I decided that the candlelight should evoke a time after guests have gone,
After they are gone with their distractions & the roses come into their own.
I decided to remember the red silk Japanese lanterns, that Christmas, that
First Christmas in Montparnasse.
I decided that lanterns are like a disguise for roses.
I decided that weight, though, was the gravamen of *these* roses, their truest
Expression of the self.
I decided that feeling has an overwhelming physical weight. Doesn't it? Not
To be confused with sickness. But just as felt as sickness. A sinking weight.
"Heavy Roses"— I will call it, I decided— call them.

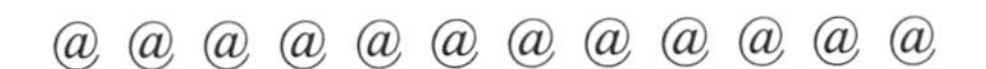

I give you:
need & depth,
swollen as fate.

A simile:
pressure like
a gaze on a path.

I give you a simile:
engorged,
tense as enemy lines.

I give you simile on top of simile:
petals
of course like tongues,

Petals like pink suns.

@ @ @ @ @ @ @ @ @ @ @ @

Thirsty roses
The gravity of roses after their thirst has been slaked
Their smell still rich as young semen
Petals
Loosening second on top of uncounted second
Moist ridges on top of the darkness
By manipulating them I touch
An infinity of selves
I fight for control

Through winding, whorling, on the edge of convulsion
Petals, petals
Petals
Shoulder shape on top of shoulder shape they drop
Continent after continent
A plotlessness impossible to fathom
Toward the scentless aftermath
The simple death I myself
Desire

@ @ @ @ @ @ @ @ @ @ @ @

24 hours later I shall brush their dried petals
Into a crisp little mound

& with my palm a mortar & my finger a pestle
Crush them, crush them fine.

By then, they will have no longer to wait, no longer, my heavy roses—
Suspended between mist & dust.

@ @ @ @ @ @ @ @ @ @ @ @

Of the twelve,
Only you still looked up
Lovesick one, one overcome by lust.
The moment dictated what I did:
The greenery wet, the attar
Expelled, a crest. What
If we were to meet
Again
O
n
c
e
m
o
r
e
p
a
l
e
w
a
r
m
t
h
?

@ @ @ @ @ @ @ @ @ @ @ @

Last Tuesday, my letter went to her, early.
I must be willing to change, mailing her that letter.

Letter on top of letter
Summer-saga
The paper open in every direction
Quavery phantom letters in lieu of petals
Down to lost time
Letter on top of letter falls under the wheels

All of her youth was bitter to remember
Her sweet rye-king sandwiches
The sticky honey
Presence
                    Absence
                                        A change of worlds

"Your indifference grows"
"My patience extenuates"

The facets of a letter refolded—
She'd have refolded the letter, her lips closed tight.

A change of worlds

A train pulling away into a far, flat land.
The brain enters into a drizzle, a continuo,

A change of worlds.
A change of worlds:

"How was it for her? Did she die easy?"
Last Thursday, or Friday, my letter went to her.

"I do not know, my friend.
I was not there."

@ @ @ @ @ @ @ @ @ @ @ @

I can name the year I had them, had taken them in, & photographed them,
The one-colored roses.
In August 1914 Germany invaded France & the War began.
I held in my hand a passage for New York from Marseilles, paper for my
Future.
Though they made their good-byes to me in the tenderest beige of the day,
They could hardly believe the going away.
Now I understand— they never wanted to be photographed, or painted
Either.
Now I think I understand— they wanted to be turned into glass,
Translucent & stained.

Snow on the Skylight All Afternoon

Weight as marble. That's how I picture— see and
Feel— myself. It helps me to keep from jiggling.
Mirror's useful. Looking in there I say Ah!
  Sculpture! She's lovely.

Students— crowded all round my platform. Seldom
Look at *them*. Just Ardensen (so I've heard him
Called). I'd say he's talented. Other than that
  None of them seems to

Grasp the *point* of art (not that *I* know what that
Is). I notice everyone's hands, especially
His. They're slender. Ring fingers on the long side.
  Graceful, erotic. . .

Doesn't watch his piece as he shapes it, keeps his
Gaze on me, I mean on the model, lets both
Hands, and eyes too, move of their own accord, true
  Sign of an artist.

When he does that, does he imagine. . . touching
Real girls? even me! or, uh, when he strokes in-
Side her thigh oh God I just moved my knee at
  Least half-a-foot, which

Irritated him, but it's *hard*, not moving.
Harder than I thought it would be. I'm *pretty*
Good at this. I do understand he needs me
  Perfectly still— he's

Trying to get me beautiful. How would I
Like to try it, like sculpting, I mean, myself.
Trouble is there's only one other girl here—
  Brita, or Brigit—

Something like that. She's not at all my type, not
Friendly, not to me, that is. Downright brassy
Toward *them*, even sasses the *teachers*. Bobs her
  Hair, well in *my* o-

Pinion, *no* girl doesn't look better with long
Hair. You couldn't *pay* me. I doubt they'd let me
In, but still, I have about half a mind to
  Ask in the office.

Plaster casts. . . down there in the basement. . . other
Evening slipped down there for a peek, I even
Touched a torso, male. Now why don't these young men
  Learn how to make me

Smooth as *that*? I thought it would feel like talcum
Powder feels when smoothed on my body. No. Felt
Much, well, harder. Cool, almost slick, I'd say. 'Course
  Plaster of Paris

Isn't like wet clay. I expect I'd hate the
Muck of actually being a sculptress, but
After all, it washes off. But I see that—
  Who's-it, Norwegian-

Sounding— Birta, I think it might be— watch her
Work, she'll pause, and squint at her figure, run her
Hands— wet clay and all— back through her hair, fingers
  Spread out like men do.

Then it dries— the clay— gets all pale and stiff, it
Stiffens something fierce in that short hair. I think
Scarecrow! She even patches her old coat, well,
  Ardensen never

Looks her way that I've ever seen. Mm. Start of
Halfway break, he picks up my wrap, his shyness
Showing, drapes it over my shoulders, nods his
  Head as if saying

Words. Mm. Think I'm due for a new kimono.
Paisley, maybe, purples and blues. It's *cold* in
Here today. Last pose of the class, thank goodness.
  What do I want for

Supper? Eggs, toast, cocoa. Yesterday evening
Went along the causeway, then past the Lion,
Caught a glimpse of Ardensen through the window,
  Draining his glass of

Wine, red wine, and just as the rim of wineglass
Left his lips, he happened to see me, looked straight
At me, eyes. . . so *liquid*, a *glance*— maybe three
  Seconds. It froze, though.

White Sands

Why am I not beautiful
  in my marigold shawl in this stark place?
    My shadow shows a woman
      with nice-shaped hair, with notebook
        held open on her knee with one hand
          while the other hand turns a page. Beautiful?
True, were there other people's shadows
  next to it for comparison,
    my shadow would show a woman
      too large to be thought attractive.
        But in the new physics' Many Worlds Interpretation,
          am I not beautiful?
Wave functions do not collapse but split:
  reality branches. When one possibility
    actualizes in one branch, the other possibility—
      what could have happened but apparently didn't—
        apparently actualizes in another branch
          (even though both exist in time).
The consciousnesses present at such a crux
  split also and have utterly no knowledge
    the one of the other
      (even though both exist in being).
        Three men have appeared on the next
          undulation's horizon. Now
I cannot make out anything they are saying.
  Now they are passing in profile. Now they are
    speaking a language I don't understand.
      When they do not look my way,
        in another world they see me: a woman
          reclining, odalisque in saffron with a notebook.

Or she is among the whoms of me they see,
    and branch and branch and branch, the sand reforms.
        In the many worlds theory, my loneliness is not definite.
            Bill Power and Joel Bettridge and Sidney Perkowitz
                sit with me, each in my turn, each
                    asking me his local question.
Will we be together again after all,
    somehow? Do you believe in me? Don't you find
        this dusk-mounded world a beautiful, a strange, place?
            I answer yes, I answer yes, wholly feminine,
                I answer yes.
                    Why am I not a deity, in my marigold shawl?

from *The Book of Brilliant Accoutrements*

Material Creativity
Has a loop of the sun for a brush.
Dürer's nature
                                        shows
Surfaces and measures all around.

Dürer's pose: a lute,
A mirror, plants in the window,
While *Melencolia* sits
In surly despondency.
                                        She
Can't make measure,
Can't feel flow; Dürer
Can make measure feel flow.
The male model he uses sits

In for the female figure.
Leyster's pose: not a lute, no,
She didn't pose
                                        a mirror
But she posed
                                        in a mirror.
Leyster coaxed a fiddler
Laughing from her palette.

Leyster has a loop of
Pictures encircling
                                        Her wrist;

Dürer has a loop of
Pictures dandled from
His belt;
Material Creativity has a loop of
The brush for a sun.

Contents

Orange Rose & Blue Reader

THERE was once an orange, orange rose who had served Father Shame well and faithfully for many years, but on account of her many wounds, could serve no longer. Father Shame said, "You can go home now. I have no further need for you, and can only pay those who serve me."

The rose did not know what to do for a living, and she went sadly away. She walked all day till she reached a broad meadow, and there in the distance she saw a light. On approaching it she found a snug cottage inhabited by Father Remembrance.

"Pray give me shelter for the night and something to eat and drink," the rose said, "or I shall perish."

"Oh ho!" Father Remembrance said. "Who gives anything to a runaway rose, I should like to know? But I will be merciful and take you in if you will do something for me."

"What is it?" asked the rose.

"I want you to dig up my garden tomorrow."

The rose agreed to this and the next day she worked as hard as she could, but she could not finish before evening.

"I see," said Father Remembrance, "that you can do no more this evening. I will keep you one night more, and tomorrow you shall clean the stove, inside and out."

The rose took the whole day over this task. In the evening Father Remembrance proposed that she should again stay another night.

"You shall only have a very light task tomorrow," he said. "There is an old dry well behind my house. My pilot light, which burns blue and never goes out, has fallen into it and I want you to bring it back."

Next day Father Remembrance led her to the well, and let her down in a basket. Sure enough, the rose found the blue flame and made a sign to be pulled up, but when she was near the top, Father Remembrance put out his hand to take the light from her.

Seeing the old man's evil designs, the rose said, "No. I will not give it to you till I have both feet safe on the ground again."

Father Remembrance flew into a rage, and let the rose fall back into the well. The poor little thing landed on very hard moss, but without being injured, and the blue flame burnt as brightly as ever. But what was the good of that? She saw that she could not escape death.

She sat for some time feeling very sad. Then, happening to put her hand into her purse, she found a little pipe a chrysanthemum had given her in another story. The pipe's bowl was still half full of weed.

'This will be my last pleasure,' she thought, as she drew the blue flame through the weed and began to smoke up. Before she knew it, she was finishing the final double drag, which she inhaled deeply, her eyes shut tight, aware of the tingling of her thorns.

When the cloud of pungent scent she had made cleared off a little, she looked up, and of all things, a handsome reader appeared over her head at the top of the well and asked, "What motions, mistress?"

"What do you mean?" the rose asked in amazement.

"I must do anything that you command," said he.

“Oh, if that is so,” said she, “get me out of this well first.”

The next thing she knew, her eyes were on a level with the reader’s. But she had not forgotten to take the light with her, under her tongue. Therefore, when he told her how he had been sad himself up to then, one dull day creeping like another, she merely nodded solemnly.

Then the handsome blue reader took the rose and led her through a corridor of wind. On the way, he showed her the autumn leaves that Father Shame and Father Remembrance had abandoned in the air. What with all these leaves, the world was like smiles all around them.

After that, often smiles were on their faces too. The reader took his time, but soon enough, he kissed the rose, whereupon she lifted her tongue. And in that moment, the reader became this book.

Well, leaves are leaves, and these leaves gave way to snow, but of course there were always more at some point or other. As for Blue Reader and Orange Rose, by and by they were married in a simple civil ceremony. What about the flame, which had given each of these two, identity and love, all at once? Why, it grew and grew and grew until the whole sky became a pilot light, cerulean in shade, consuming the sun for years to come.

Letters

Once upon a time
I don't know how you meant me to feel
But frankly how happy you nonetheless did make me feel
When you wrote to me

About the first day of classes
How it was strange to see the door to "my" office, open and lit,
Tuesday early.
How could I not find mystery— not even so much

In the word "strange" there— as in
The "somehow" in your next sentence:
"I somehow expected to find you there."
Tuesday early.

Tuesday early.
With or without words.
Thursday early.
The sound of your key in the door across the way.

I remember I said to the sound of the water fountain once,
"Joseph, is that you?"
"Yes." Your voice. And you appeared in my doorway saying
"So you're staying in town this week?"

I replied "yes, thank God"; in the middle of my job search
And in nervousness at your presence, I lost ahold of
Whatever scrap of paper was in my hand.
A scrap of paper, like a bookmark, on the floor.

Then seven time zones away, you in Barcelona,
Listening to that singer, sing. Schubert. Finzi. And lightly in the encore—
This you found amusing—
"If Ever I Should Leave You," from *Camelot.*

I wrote to you: "Have you met your new colleague, then?"
While I half hummed, half pronounced lyrics: *It wouldn't be in autumn. . .*
I'd thought I might, in departing, place with my successor
A robin's feather I'd picked up west of the library.

Or better, a piece of paper recording the dimensions of Thoreau's cabin
Where it stood up-rise from Walden Pond.
But inside the actual little office, I could tell that my aura or
Whatever it can be called

Had drained, already, completely, away.
Of course I couldn't be leaving feathers or notes to a perfect stranger
Who just happened to come into a space that I loved,
For my year, to inhabit.

Bill Demastes, expecting the new person to arrive any day,
Was hooking up the new computer on the new desk busily.
I thought, 'Good-bye, once my space.'
But under the language, it was you. Joseph.

Now will you understand why
I didn't want you muttering 'you shouldn't have'
In reference to the simple bag of coffee
I left you that day.

Skin

Uncurl the sheet of vellum and there

Are the obscurely interrupted complex roses,
The letters of English,
The vine with a thousand ears,
The decay of the tempera and the decay of the vegetative shell,
The decay of addition, of cracking, and air with its vigor,
Which grinds or is perhaps shifted away
Like the day.
Uncurl the sheets, there is in them the decay of the trembling recorder,
The decay of the dipping hands, of the chant, of the anvil in the ear,
The decay of the swallow-like bell-tolls, bolting from the tower.
Did the scrivener will with one's utter heart the snail's-pace risk?
Catch it in the bell sound? smell it in the domicile rain?
To love the thin vellums and the erasure, scraping on them. . .
To love anything,
You must be prepared to rip, or bear its trace.

THE IOWA POETRY PRIZE & EDWIN FORD PIPER POETRY AWARD WINNERS

1987
Elton Glaser, *Tropical Depressions*
Michael Pettit, *Cardinal Points*

1988
Bill Knott, *Outremer*
Mary Ruefle, *The Adamant*

1989
Conrad Hilberry, *Sorting the Smoke*
Terese Svoboda, *Laughing Africa*

1990
Philip Dacey,
Night Shift at the Crucifix Factory
Lynda Hull, *Star Ledger*

1991
Greg Pape, *Sunflower Facing the Sun*
Walter Pavlich,
Running near the End of the World

1992
Lola Haskins, *Hunger*
Katherine Soniat, *A Shared Life*

1993
Tom Andrews,
The Hemophiliac's Motorcycle
Michael Heffernan, *Love's Answer*
John Wood, *In Primary Light*

1994
James McKean, *Tree of Heaven*
Bin Ramke, *Massacre of the Innocents*
Ed Roberson,
Voices Cast Out to Talk Us In

1995
Ralph Burns, *Swamp Candles*
Maureen Seaton, *Furious Cooking*

1996
Pamela Alexander, *Inland*
Gary Gildner,
The Bunker in the Parsley Fields
John Wood,
The Gates of the Elect Kingdom

1997
Brendan Galvin, *Hotel Malabar*
Leslie Ullman, *Slow Work through Sand*

1998
Kathleen Peirce, *The Oval Hour*
Bin Ramke, *Wake*
Cole Swensen, *Try*

1999
Larissa Szporluk, *Isolato*
Liz Waldner,
A Point Is That Which Has No Part

2000
Mary Leader, *The Penultimate Suitor*